How to Get an A grade

Edexcel AS Ethics and Philosophy of Religion

Laura Mears

First published 2014 by PushMe Press

Mid Somerset House, Southover, Wells, Somerset BA5 1UH

www.pushmepress.com

© 2014 Inducit Learning Ltd

British Library Cataloguing in Publication Data
A catalogue record for this book is available from the British Library

ISBN: 978-1-909618-58-9 (pbk)
ISBN: 978-1-910252-86-4 (hbk)
ISBN: 978-1-910252-82-6 (ebk)
ISBN: 978-1-910252-83-3 (pdf)

Typeset in Frutiger by booksellerate.com
Printed by Lightning Source

Disclaimer

Edexcel, a product of Pearson Education Ltd, accepts no responsibility for the accuracy or method of working in the answers given.

Contents

Introduction...1

What are exams for?..3

How to analyse the specification........................7

How to analyse past exam questions.....................37

How to prepare for the examination.......................79

Revision tips...99

Postscript..103

A rich and engaging community assisted by the best teachers in Philosophy

philosophy.pushmepress.com

Students and teachers explore Philosophy of Religion through handouts, film clips, presentations, case studies, extracts, games and academic articles.

Pitched just right, and so much more than a textbook, here is a place to engage with critical reflection whatever your level. Marked student essays are also posted.

Introduction

Achieving the A grade is a bit like achieving a win in the world of sport.

It is not enough to have a team of talented players who have a high level of skill and determination to succeed.

My father is a basketball coach and recently his team, the Cheshire Phoenix, lost by one point in extra time to top-of-the-league Worcester Wolves. After a few sleepless nights he developed a defensive tactic which was the perfect match for the Wolves' seemingly unbeatable offensive. The skill of his players, along with the right tactic to suit the opposition, gave his team the confidence they needed to meet their next Worcester encounter.

In the same way, it is not enough to have a sound knowledge of scholars, terminology, issues and debates within Philosophy and Ethics. Although these things are essential for the A grade, on their own they cannot guarantee success. What is also needed is a developed set of tactics ready to employ for any question type. Only then can the hope of an A grade become a likelihood.

In this book, I have gathered and prepared a feast of top tips and tactics so that you can enter the exam hall with the confidence that you can handle any question the examiners throw your way. I have drawn on past papers, mark schemes, examiners' reports and my years of experience as a teacher of A level Religious Studies. Pore over it, devour it, drill it and hone it, and together with rigorous revision of the material, you will be well placed to achieve your goal of an A grade.

Laura Mears

What are exams for?

Is there a reason for exams; a philosophy behind the subject you are doing?

The answer is "yes", and it helps if you understand the philosophy behind Philosophy and Ethics, because in the end, if you become a philosopher and can show this in the exam, you should gain close to full marks.

The word philosophy means "a love of wisdom", and we gain wisdom by exercising a special type of thinking skill. The Greeks believed this skill was a foundational skill, because thinking well was a key to living well. So, we might ask, how do we "think well"?

I was encouraged recently to hear of a school which has a cookie club which meets at 4pm every week on a Thursday. The idea of the cookie club is to meet and debate - or if you like, to argue a case. Sometimes a member of staff, and sometimes a student, comes with a case to defend, and everyone has to argue against the point of view that person is defending.

Something like this underlies the subject of philosophy. Philosophy is about presenting, arguing and then defending a case. So, for example, Plato uses a method of dispute in his writing called the Socratic method, where he puts words into the mouth of an adversary and then proceeds to dispute and disprove that opponent's case.

Of course this begs some questions.

WHAT DO I ACTUALLY BELIEVE ABOUT, SAY, GAY MARRIAGE?

I awarded a prize recently to anyone who could provide a good philosophical case against gay marriage. I announced the prize at a conference, and I guess it was no surprise that the speaker next to me murmured "there isn't one".

The speaker is, of course, wrong. The problem is, we sometimes need moral courage to oppose a view which most people hold. If I (for the sake of argument) oppose gay marriage, some people might call me a homophobe; other people may describe me as a right-wing fundamentalist, out of tune with reality.

But philosophers should not worry about this, because philosophy is concerned with the nature and strength of arguments, and nothing else. People can cause me to take poison like Socrates had to, they can insult me in newspapers and they can walk out of conferences. But we need to hold steadfastly to this point: social welfare only proceeds by the analysis and evaluation of arguments. It is only by this process that any great social reform has come. Bad arguments produce bad politics and bad policies; good arguments do the opposite.

In your A level, have the courage to present and then own for yourself good, strong, well-justified arguments and you will be on the way to an A grade.

WHAT MAKES AN ARGUMENT WEAK?

A weak argument can really only be of two types. It can be logically unsound. And it can be factually unsound. Some arguments may present both weaknesses.

For example, consider this argument:

1. The world is either flat or square.

2. The world is not flat.

3. So the world must be square.

What is wrong with this? Well, it is false in two senses. First it commits a logical mistake - of restricting the options. It only gives us a choice of two possibilities, flat or square, when in fact there are many possible shapes, and the correct answer (the world is round) isn't given as a possibility.

Second, it is empirically or factually false. As a matter of fact, if I set off in my little sailing boat and head west (assuming I remember to navigate for the Panama Canal) I will eventually end up where I started. So I can attack the argument on two grounds, the logical and the factual, making clear what my two grounds are.

What about this argument about abortion?

1. The foetus resembles a human being at 11 weeks.

2. Human beings have feelings, thoughts and desires.

3. Therefore a foetus has feelings, thoughts and desires at 11 weeks.

What is wrong with this argument? It actually begs a question, or perhaps begs two questions. Is resembling a human being enough to infer that something is a human being? After all, statues, dolls and toy soldiers all resemble human beings, but that doesn't mean they are human beings.

Second, it lists a number of things that human beings do: they feel, think and want things. These may be necessary conditions for being human - it's hard to imagine a human being, except one in a persistent vegetative state, that doesn't at least have feelings. But is that list sufficient for defining a human being? After all my dog feels, thinks and wants its walk at 8am, but I wouldn't call my dog human.

Some facts are important for ethics. It is morally important where we can establish beyond doubt that the planet is warming. It is morally important whether a foetus feels pain (estimates range from 18 to 26 weeks) and at what stage of development. It is morally important in IVF treatment to know how many cycles a woman is allowed on the NHS and what the chances of success are, as these raise questions of rights and justice. Is it fair that my hospital excludes women over 37 from treatment? It is morally important to know who suffers when the company Trafigura dumps toxic waste in the Ivory Coast and how much compensation the inhabitants deserve for their suffering.

But, of course, we must check the facts. Bad facts produce bad ethics - and it wasn't long ago that some people were arguing that certain races were less intelligent than others, as a monstrous argument for discrimination, well considered in the 2012 film on President Lincoln.

How to analyse the specification

UNIT 1 FOUNDATIONS (EDEXCEL 6RS01)

The Edexcel specification for Unit 1 is broad, with the intention of trying to reward knowledge and understanding of a number of debates and areas within a topic, rather than testing the candidate's grasp of one particular scholar or angle. This is good news! If you have enjoyed and explored Peter Singer's ideas about utilitarianism in particular, you will always be able to talk about them in any question on utilitarianism, because, unlike in other exam boards, the question will never be confined to, for example, a comparison between Bentham and Mill. Where some understanding of a particular philosopher's contribution is expected or advised (as with Augustine and Aquinas in the area of Just War Theory), names are given.

However, for some given topics, few or no specific scholars are mentioned. Where this is the case, I have tried to suggest which philosophers may provide scope for a helpful discussion on the topic in question. The important thing to remember is that, whether or not the specification mentions specific scholars, it is expected that your response will be rich in reference to the works of relevant scholars - both supporters of the theory, and as critics.

To be an A-grade scholar you need to:

- Have a clear grasp of what the specification asks for generally, for each part of the question, for example, a thorough use of philosophical terminology.

- Have a clear grasp of what the specification asks for specifically, for each topic area. For example, the contributions of Hume to the debate about miracles.

The pages that follow will lead you in a study of these two considerations - general and specific.

Candidates have 1 hour and 45 minutes to answer **THREE QUESTIONS** from **AT LEAST TWO DIFFERENT** areas of study. Most centres teach material from Philosophy of Religion and Ethics, but either could be taught alongside New Testament, or one of the six major world religions. It is also possible to answer **ONE QUESTION** from **EACH OF THREE AREAS** of study.

For Unit 1, the specification indicates that the following skills and aptitudes are desirable:

- knowledge and understanding of key concepts and terminology within the topic area, written in a fluent, well-structured and coherent style

- the background to a theory or issue, such as the historical or philosophical context

- specific and detailed knowledge of key thinkers, sources and critics within the area of study, including relevant examples, quotations and references to their teachings and texts

- an ability to relate debates to more general issues within religion, human experience and the wider world

- a clearly expressed and reasoned point of view, achieved through assessing the extent to which the arguments stand up to scrutiny.

Each question is broken down into two parts, part (i) and part (ii).

PART (i) AO1 - KNOWLEDGE AND UNDERSTANDING

In the first part of the question, which carries the most marks (21/30), you will need to fulfil the first four of the five bullet points above. Start with a concise introduction that sets out clearly where you are going.

Examiner Tip: Show in the introduction that the answer will follow the pattern of the question set in a structured way, and deal with the evidence.

Your answer should be dense with terminology, scholarship, quotation and example, clearly identifying the most important features of the problem or argument under consideration.

The mark scheme asks for ideas to be explored

at a wide range or considerable depth.

This means you can choose either to look at a number of issues and arguments, or one in detail. But if you choose to do the latter, be careful to look at a number of contributors to that argument, rather than continually quoting from the same scholar.

The mark scheme also asks for the A grader to write

Concisely ... cogently ...

This means that your sentences should be rich with detail. Here is an example from the problem of evil:

This creates problems for religious believers, summed up in JL Mackie's "Inconsistent Triad", which questions God's omnipotence and benevolence in the presence of evil.

This sentence is concise because it contains at least three key terms, as well as reference to a scholar.

You can further improve your writing by ensuring that one paragraph flows from another through the use of link words and phrases, such as:

- In extension

- By contrast

- A further consideration

- Building on the work of ...

- Yet ...

- Furthermore ...

As the specification does not ask for certain scholars to be studied as compulsory elements, the question will not make reference to particular thinkers. You will not, therefore, be asked to "Give an account of Jeremy Bentham's version of utilitarianism" or "Identify the key differences between the Augustinian and Irenaean approaches to the problem of evil". Rather, the questions will be more general to the topic as a whole, beginning with trigger words from a list contained in the syllabus:

- Compare

- Describe

- Examine

- Give an account of

- How

- Identify

- Illustrate

- In what ways

- Outline

- Select

- What

Strengths and weaknesses

A discussion of strengths and weaknesses will usually come in part (i), and it is necessary to include this, even if it is not explicitly asked for in the terms of the question. A good way to prepare for this is to draw up tables of strengths and weaknesses for each of the arguments or defences proposed. It is important to link as many strengths or weaknesses as you can with a philosopher, preferably with a quotation. This gives much more weight to your well-reasoned points.

The difference between "examine" and "evaluate"

This list stops short of using the word "evaluate" because that is reserved for part (ii). However, examination of the arguments and their strengths and weaknesses is needed for part (i).

Here you should put forward strengths, weaknesses and critique; distinguish between strong and weak approaches, and show developments and improvements to the argument in question, such as how Mill's version of utilitarianism solves the problem of distinguishing between higher and lower pleasures. For example, you can use phrases like:

- Possibly the strongest objection to the argument is ...

- Yet perhaps the most convincing criticism is ...

- A major improvement to the theory may have come in the shape of ...

Such phrases will hugely aid the coherence and flow of your essay, as it moves from part (i) to part (ii). However, keep focused on the question in part (i), and save your evaluation for part (ii).

PART (ii) AO2 - EVALUATION

This part carries just 9/30 marks, but it is crucial in the pursuit of an A grade. Imagine you score really highly on part (i), (19/21), but save little time for evaluation. Many answers to part (ii) do not make it out of level 2, scoring only 4/9.

(Ask your teacher for a copy of the one-page level descriptors on page 117 of the syllabus, or download your own copy from the Edexcel website.) A total score of 23/30 will yield a mere (but high) B grade. How frustrating!

Trigger words for part (ii) are:

- Analyse

- Compare and contrast

- Differentiate

- Distinguish between

- Define

- Examine

- Explain

Yet perhaps the most helpful phrase is the one found in the level descriptors:

Critically evaluate and justify a point of view through the use of evidence and reasoned argument.

Steer clear of repeating or simply churning out knowledge and understanding of scholars and arguments here. It may be appropriate to introduce something new, but do this concisely, and in support of your point of view. Here is an example:

> *Although I have clearly shown why I think there are major flaws in each Design Argument when viewed in isolation, I believe that a cumulative approach may provide a way forward. Swinburne's "leaky bucket" analogy is helpful here. He argued that placing a series of leaky buckets one in another may hold water where each individual bucket cannot. It is my opinion that together with other arguments for the existence of God, such as cosmological and moral ones, the Design Arguments as a whole can be said to make a valid contribution in support of the justification for God's existence.*

It does not matter what your point of view is, so long as you have considered the arguments critically (looking at strengths and weaknesses). Try to stay off the fence! Instead, if your mind is not made up firmly one way or the other, find a middle ground to call your own, such as proportionalism in Ethics, or deism with regard to the cosmological argument in the Philosophy of Religion.

UNIT 1 AS PHILOSOPHY OF RELIGION

There is no additional advice for Philosophy of Religion essays, but applying the skills and aptitudes above, one might like to consider including:

- broad categories about the argument, for example, whether the theory is empirical or rational; a posteriori or a priori; and whether it uses deductive or inductive reasoning

- relating the debate to issues about God's existence: atheism, agnosticism, theism or deism, and the nature of God as omnipotent, omniscient, omnibenevolent, etc.

Candidates should be able to demonstrate knowledge and understanding of **AT LEAST ONE** and **UP TO TWO** of the following areas of study.

The arguments from design/teleological arguments

Candidates should be able to demonstrate knowledge and understanding of:

- the nature of the arguments as empirical, based on experience or analogy and interpretation

- some teleological arguments from key contributors, such as Aquinas, Paley, Tennant and Swinburne

- key strengths and weaknesses of the arguments, drawing on contributions from critics such as Hume, Mill, Kant, Darwin and Dawkins

- the need to state clearly to what extent the arguments and their criticisms succeed or fail, and how that affects debates about God's existence.

The cosmological arguments

Candidates should be able to demonstrate knowledge and understanding of:

- the nature of the arguments as empirical, based on the observation of cause and effect in the universe

- some cosmological arguments from key contributors, such as Aquinas, Kalaam philosophers, Leibniz and Copleston

- key strengths and weaknesses of the arguments, drawing on contributions from critics such as Hume, Kant and Russell, as well as wider debates about necessary existence, brute facts and infinite regression

- the need to state clearly to what extent the arguments and their criticisms succeed or fail, and where that leaves the concept of God.

The problems of evil and suffering

Candidates should be able to demonstrate knowledge and understanding of:

- the key concepts and terms surrounding this issue, such as moral and natural (non-moral) evil, vale of soul-making, best of all possible worlds, free-will defence, the meaning of the term "theodicy", and what's at stake concerning the nature of God (Mackie's inconsistent triad may be helpful here)

- some theodicies and defences of God's existence or nature from key areas of scholarship, such as Augustine, Irenaeus, Hick, Swinburne, process theology and the free-will defence

- strengths and weaknesses of the arguments, drawing on contributions from critics such as Hume, Kant, Schleiermacher, Mill, Flew, Russell and Dawkins

- the need to state clearly to what extent the arguments and their criticisms succeed or fail, and where that leaves the existence and/or nature of God.

Miracles

Candidates should be able to demonstrate knowledge and understanding of:

- different definitions of the term miracle, and their connection with the attributes of, and belief in, God

- other scholars associated with debates about miracles, such as Locke, Holland, Moore, Swinburne, Wiles.

Hume may be identified in questions, so he is the only compulsory scholar for this topic. Biblical material may be drawn on, but keep it relevant to the making of a philosophical point.

Remember the need to state clearly your personal view on how to define the term miracle, the likelihood of miraculous occurrences, and the nature of God in reference to this debate.

TECHNICAL VOCABULARY

The Edexcel syllabus contains no glossary of terms, but the specification repeatedly refers to the need for a range of technical vocabulary. It is best to prepare a list of terms, along with definitions, and learn them thoroughly. A meal made without seasoning can be tasteless and bland. Likewise, a good peppering of technical vocabulary will go a long way towards convincing the examiner that you have prepared thoroughly and have a developed grasp of the issues at stake.

If you need further convincing, it is worth saying that the phrase "using a range of technical vocabulary" is deployed both for part (i) and part (ii), so you get double the credit!

Such a list may include the following terms, but you will need to add your own, as well as the definitions from your textbooks and notes.

- Atheism

- Agnosticism

- Analogy

- Anthropomorphism

- A posteriori

- Coincidence

- Contingency

- Cosmological

- Creatio ex nihilo

- Deism

- Empiricism

- Foreknowledge

- Impossible

- Inductive reasoning

- Laws of nature

- Necessary existence

- Omnibenevolence

- Omnipotence

- Omniscience

- Predestination

- Reductio ad absurdum

- Teleological

- Theism

- Theodicy

UNIT 1 AS ETHICS

There is no additional advice for Ethics essays, but applying the skills and aptitudes above, one might like to consider including:

- broad categories about the argument, for example, whether the theory is deontological or teleological, absolutist or relativist, objective or subjective

- relating the debate to issues about the nature and role of religion in issues of morality, law-making, social action and the media.

Candidates should be able to demonstrate knowledge and understanding of **AT LEAST ONE** and **UP TO TWO** of the following areas of study.

The relationship between religion and morality

Candidates should be able to demonstrate knowledge and understanding of:

- the nature of, and background to, the debate; secularism and the unification of church and state

- some religious perspectives on morality, such as Divine Command Theory, Situation Ethics or ideas about a moral law-giver, conscience and the need for objectivity within ethics

- key strengths and weaknesses of the arguments, drawing on the Euthyphro Dilemma, difficult passages of scripture "such as God's command to sacrifice Isaac (Genesis 22) or the teaching of the Westboro Baptist Church" (quoted from p52 of the specification)

- the need to state clearly to what extent the arguments and their criticisms succeed or fail, and how that affects your view on how religion and morality could or should be connected.

Utilitarianism

Candidates should be able to demonstrate knowledge and understanding of:

- the background to the theory; its emergence in a climate of post-enlightenment thinking, the industrial revolution and social philanthropy

- key terminology, arguments and scholars from some of the main versions including Act and Rule Utilitarianism, Bentham and Mill, and one or more of the modern developments including Ideal (GE Moore), Preference (Peter Singer) and Negative Utilitarianism

- key strengths and weaknesses of the arguments, drawing on, for example, deontological objections to teleological theories, as well as more specific criticisms

- the need to state clearly to what extent the arguments and their criticisms succeed or fail, and your consequent point of view on the success of this theory as a guide in ethical decision-making.

Situation Ethics

Candidates should be able to demonstrate knowledge and understanding of:

- the social and cultural background to the theory; its emergence in the post-war 20th C and its climate of sexual liberation, feminism, civil rights and secularism

- contributions and quotations from original source material from the main contributors, JAT Robinson and Joseph Fletcher

- key strengths, weaknesses and criticisms from thinkers including William Barclay (Ethics in a Permissive Society), drawing on examples without allowing case studies to dominate

- the need to state clearly to what extent the arguments and their criticisms succeed or fail, and your consequent point of view on the success of this theory as a guide in ethical decision-making.

War and peace

Candidates should be able to demonstrate knowledge and understanding of:

- a detailed scrutiny of Just War Theory, with reference to Augustine and Aquinas and additional thinkers on the theory if desired

- religious and non-religious justifications for pacifism, drawing on the work of relevant organisations, and individuals, such as the teachings of Jesus

- key strengths and weaknesses of Just War Theory and pacificism, with concise reference to recent or contemporary wars

- the need to state clearly to what extent the arguments and their criticisms succeed or fail, and your consequent point of view on whether these approaches help with decisions about war and peace, and the state of the world in which we live.

Sexual ethics

Candidates should be able to demonstrate knowledge and understanding of:

- a range of issues within sexual morality, including marital, non-marital and extra-marital sex, homosexuality and divorce; reference to related issues such as abortion or IVF should only be explored with relevance to sexual ethics

- religious and non-religious approaches to these issues, including religious teachings and texts, absolute or relative approaches such as Situation Ethics

- key strengths and weaknesses of religious and non-religious approaches, with reference to scholars; these could include Peter Singer, John Stott, Peter Vardy and John Wyatt (suggested in the further resources and support appendix of the specification)

- the need to state clearly which approaches you consider to be most helpful in individual and communal decision-making, and what sort of society you would see emerging as a result of your findings.

TECHNICAL VOCABULARY

As with Philosophy of Religion, I have included a suggested list, but you may need to add to it, as well as the definitions gathered from your textbooks and notes.

- Absolute

- Adultery

- Agapeism

- Conscientious objector

- Consequentialist

- Fidelity

- Deontological

- Hedonic calculus

- Normative ethics

- Objective

- Pacifism

- Proportion

- Relative

- Secularism

- Subjective

- Teleologicalism

UNIT 2 INVESTIGATIONS (EDEXCEL 6RS02)

Candidates have 1 hour and 15 minutes to answer **ONE QUESTION** from their selected area of study. Some centres teach one topic, and all candidates write their own variations; some centres let their students loose on the syllabus. This means there will be a varying level of support and guidance from centres, so it is important to be aware of some of the main things the examiners are looking for, no matter which topic is selected.

For Unit 2, the specification indicates that the following skills and aptitudes are desirable:

- knowledge and understanding of key concepts and terminology within the topic area, written in a fluent, well-structured and coherent style

- a wide range of well-selected source material including relevant examples and factual knowledge which supports understanding of the significant features of the topic investigated, and offers some analysis of the issues raised by the topic

- specific and detailed knowledge of key thinkers, sources and supporters within the area of study, appropriate quotations and references to their teachings and texts

- a detailed consideration of the reasons for alternative views to the dominant ones presented, best presented through careful analysis

- a clearly expressed point of view, supported by well-deployed evidence and reasoned argument.

You may also wish to:

- demonstrate an awareness of the cultural, social and religious background to the issue

- show an ability to relate debates to more general issues within religion, human experience and the wider world.

The question is structured in the same way as Unit 1, with 35/50 for A01 (knowledge and understanding) and 15/50 for A02 (evaluation). The same principles apply to how to structure your answer, and what to include where, so do review the general information at the beginning of the Unit 1 section.

All questions use the phrase "with reference to the topic you have studied", so be sure to state in the introduction which topic you have chosen to focus on, and be wary of choosing too many, which may result in a very general and shallow investigation.

Area B - Philosophy of Religion

▶ **Religious experience; meditation**

Candidates should be able to demonstrate knowledge and understanding of:

- key terms within the area of study, as well as the context for religious experiences, such as cultural influences

- particular examples associated with the subject area, such as conversion, prayer and meditation across a range of religious traditions; biblical material may be drawn on, but keep it relevant to the making of a philosophical point

- scholars associated with the subject area, such as James, Otto and Hardy

- critics of religious experiences, and alternative approaches, such as the charge that these experiences are merely subjective and can be explained naturalistically

- the need to state clearly your personal view on whether an objective approach to religious experiences can be justified, and how your findings reflect insights about human nature and God.

KEY WORDS may include:

- Conversion
- Naturalism
- Numinous
- Revelation
- Transcendence

▸ **Contrasting standpoints on the relationship between mind and body**

Candidates should be able to demonstrate knowledge and understanding of:

- key terms within the area of study, and issues related to them; such terms may include: dualism, monism, disembodied consciousness and physicalism

- standpoints drawn from contrasting ideas in Western and/or Eastern Philosophy of Religion, such as interpretations of the soul and personal identity; examples may be Atman in Hinduism and Anatta in Buddhism.

I also recommend you include:

- scholars associated with the subject area, such as Aristotle, Plato and Kant, and critics such as Ryle, Dawkins and Russell

- a clear statement of your personal view on the connection and interaction between mind/soul and body, and how your findings reflect insights about human nature and God.

▸ **A study of one or more philosophers of religion**

Candidates should be able to demonstrate knowledge and understanding of contributions to the Philosophy of Religion from a key scholar such as:

- Ayer
- Aquinas
- Bonhoeffer

- Buber

- Descartes

- Hume

- Kierkegaard

- Nagarjuna

- Plato

- Sartre

- Shankara

Selecting a key idea as a focal point may be helpful. Ideas include "God" in Descartes' philosophy, or a particular text such as Hume's Natural History of Religion.

You should maintain a line of argument and head towards a clear point of view on the significance of the scholars' contributions to the wider area of Philosophy of Religion.

I also recommend you include other scholars who have contributed to, been influenced by, or held views in contrast to your chosen scholar's contributions.

Area C - The Study of Ethics

▸ Medical ethics

Candidates should be able to demonstrate knowledge and understanding of:

- Key terms and debates within their chosen area(s), selected from the following list:

    1. abortion
    2. euthanasia
    3. contraception
    4. genetic engineering
    5. organ transplantation
    6. fertility treatment
    7. development of new medical treatments and procedures

- particular examples and case studies associated with the subject area(s), although steer clear of great chunks of narrative on previous or current cases

- scholars and ethical perspectives, for example utilitarianism, religious ethics and deontological approaches, from a range of contributors

- ethical questions relating to one or more issues in medical ethics, such as the sanctity of life, medical consent, rights and duties, responsibilities and choices

- the need to state clearly your personal view on whether a religious or secular opinion can be justified in relation to your chosen area(s); a recognition of the impact of your opinions on the whole area of medical ethics, society and religious institutions.

KEY TERMS may include:

- Choices
- Medical consent
- Rights and duties
- Sanctity of life

▶ **The natural world**

Candidates should be able to demonstrate knowledge and understanding of:

- key terms and debates within their chosen area(s), selected from the following list:

  1. environmental pollution

  2. global warming

  3. deforestation and farming methods

  4. extinction and endangerment of species

  5. issues raised by recycling and other environmentally friendly lifestyle choices

  6. habitat conservation

7. national and international environmental initiatives and the relationship of animals to man, for example zoos, circuses, hunting and the use of animals in research

- particular examples and case studies associated with the subject area(s), although steer clear of great chunks of narrative on previous or current cases

- scholars and ethical perspectives, for example utilitarianism, religious ethics and deontological approaches, from a range of contributors.

I also recommend that you include a clear statement of your personal view on which religious or secular ethical approach(es) provide(s) the best way forward in your chosen area(s), and the effects this may have on the environment, and the individual and corporate moral climate.

KEY TERMS may include:

- Economic considerations
- Humanitarianism
- Responsibility
- Stewardship

▶ Equality in the modern world

Candidates should be able to demonstrate knowledge and understanding of:

- key terms and debates within their chosen area(s) of sexual and racial equality, such as homosexual partnerships and matters arising from adoption, surrogacy, same-sex parents, the nature of marriage and civil partnerships, homosexual clergy, homophobia

- issues of gender equality: feminism, sexism in the workplace and family; women leaders in the Church

- issues of racial equality: prejudices and discrimination, black-white relations, civil rights, issues surrounding Muslim relations with the West.

I also recommend you include:

- particular examples and case studies associated with the subject area(s), although steer clear of great chunks of narrative on previous or current cases

- scholars and ethical perspectives, for example utilitarianism, religious ethics and deontological approaches, from a range of contributors

- quotations from key religious and secular texts, leaders and thinkers, such as the Qur'an, the Bible, the works of classical scholars and Eastern religious texts.

The need to state clearly your personal view on whether a religious or secular opinion can be justified in relation to your chosen area(s); a recognition of the impact of your opinions on the whole area of ethics, the make-up of society and the face of religious institutions.

KEY TERMS may include:

- Civil partnerships
- Discrimination
- Headship
- Parity
- Prejudice
- Separation of roles

How to analyse past exam questions

UNIT 1 FOUNDATIONS (EDEXCEL 6RS01)

Exam board regulations mean we are unable to reproduce the exact wording of past questions, but they are so broad and repetitive that the following lists should be sufficient; "i" and "ii" refer to parts of questions.

Design argument - part (i) analysis

▸ **"Key ideas" questions (also termed "fundamental ideas")**

In exams Jan2009, Jun2010, Jan2012, Jun2012 (purpose), Jan2013

With a popular (i) question asking for a discussion about the key ideas associated with the argument from design, there is really no excuse for failing to have a plan up your sleeve for how to approach this. The knack is making sure you fulfil all of the general criteria for a level 4 A01 answer (flow of argument, scholars, examples, terminology), while showing the examiner that you have structured your response around the demands of the question.

Do not forget to include a concise introduction (see the "how to prepare for the examination" section for ideas). You may wish to prepare for this question in the following way:

Start by brainstorming all of the main ideas associated with the design argument, for example:

The Fundamental Ideas of the Design Arguments:

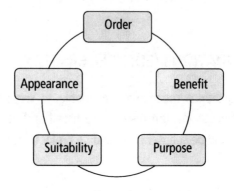

Next, link your key ideas with the work of a scholar or scholars:

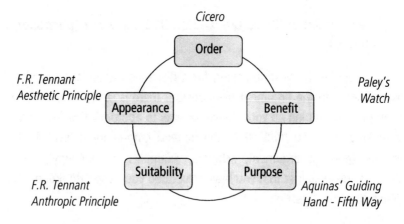

Continue in this way, by building on your plan with details, dates, quotations and links with similar ideas, then add strengths and weaknesses associated with each.

For example, a strength of the idea of "purpose" as seen in Aquinas's guiding hand principle might be its use of analogy, which makes it accessible. However, in criticism, Richard Dawkins has questioned whether a more appropriate analogy might be that of a heat-seeking missile - suggesting that rather than being shaped or fitted by a supreme being, purpose is a quality of things that is pulled from the need to survive, reproduce and adapt to the environment.

▸ One to watch ...

The January 2012 paper asked for the candidate to examine three key terms from the following list:

- Analogy

- Anthropic principle

- Design qua purpose

- Empirical evidence

- Regularities of succession

While these terms do not appear specifically in the specification, and therefore it is possible that a student may not have focused or even come across all of these phrases, you should be familiar with **AT LEAST THREE** of these concepts if you have prepared thoroughly. Add them now to your vocabulary list, and learn their meanings and contexts, just in case this question comes up again!

Please note that the question does not ask for a certain number of key ideas. Three may be ample when dealt with in detail. Likewise, more than five may be appropriate, so long as your answer does not read as a long list, and has relevant detail. The June 2012 question asked the candidate to consider "explanation of purpose" as the main role of the design argument. It is important here to talk about this role, but also to consider other roles or facets of the arguments, such as explanation of beauty (aesthetic principle). If you follow the plan outlined here, you will now have an excellent basis from which to write a well-informed response to this common question.

▸ "Strengths" questions

In exams Jan2009, Jun2009, Jan2010, Jun2013

A similar approach can be taken in preparing for a part (i) question about strengths and weaknesses.

Again, you need to make sure you fulfil all of the general criteria for a level 4 A01 answer (flow of argument, scholars, examples, terminology), while showing the examiner that you have structured your response around the demands of the question. This time, however, begin with the strengths, and structure your answer around these, for example:

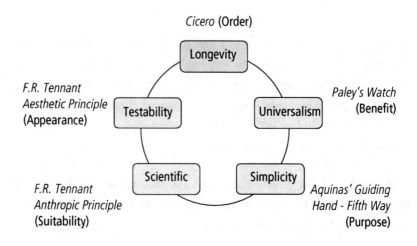

I tell my students to remember an **ACRONYM** so they don't get flustered in an examination and repeat themselves or get muddled and blur distinctions. **SLUTS** is an unattractive word, but it does the trick! The five strengths given here are triggers for you to discuss some reasons why the design arguments are still being discussed today (despite many scholars believing that in the post-Darwinian age, the design argument should be long gone). It is not enough just to list them; you must go into some detail about what you mean by the term you have used, and why you consider it a strength of the argument, preferably linking it with a scholar, text or bigger idea.

For example, consider the strength of "simplicity". You could argue that the simplest answer to the question "why do things appear to be designed?" is that they are! This reasonable explanation tallies with Ockham's Razor, which advises us not to "multiply entities beyond necessity". In other words, if God explains the evidence of design (and this is a complete explanation - link with Leibniz's Principle of Sufficient Reason), then why look elsewhere, to other, more complex explanations?

▸ **"Weaknesses" questions**

In exams Jun2009, Jan2010, Jan2011

If a part (i) question asks for a discussion of the weaknesses of the argument, it is tempting to rattle through a pre-learned essay plan which has a short, tagged-on "weaknesses/criticisms" paragraph at the end. Another, more unusual, mistake would be to just concentrate the whole essay on weaknesses, and ignore the general demands of the specification (see the "How to analyse the specific demands of the question" section in this book).

Proceeding with the same logic we have applied thus far, the A-grader may wish to structure the whole answer around the weaknesses of the argument, while failing to neglect the other important ingredients.

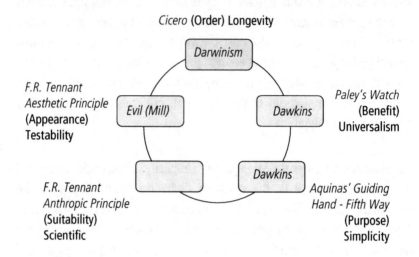

Design argument - part (ii) analysis

▸ **Strengths and weaknesses questions**
  In exams Jan2009, Jun2010, Jan2011, Jun2011

Where these occur for part (ii), the mark scheme makes it clear that you need to decide whether the strengths outweigh the weaknesses, or vice versa. A third position is where a candidate may decide that the strengths and weaknesses are equally balanced, and here the mark scheme makes it clear that you should:

"Consider the implications arising from arguments that are thought to be equally balanced."

What does this mean?

- **Questions which link the argument to the existence of God**

  In exams Jun2009, Jan2010, Jun2010, Jun2011, Jan2012(leads to valid conclusion), Jun2012(successful as proof), Jan2013(explanation for universe), Jun2013(fail to prove)

As this discussion takes place within a debate about the existence of God, then I think it will be helpful here to link certain conclusions with beliefs (pay careful attention to the specific terms of the question). Hence, for the conclusion above, it will be fair to say that the design arguments would not convince a non-believer to believe, nor give added strength to a believer's already-existing faith. Neither, however, would the weaknesses challenge the faith of a believer, nor add conviction to a sceptic's non-belief.

Cosmological argument - part (i) analysis

As you can see from the list above, there are only two main types of part (i) question: those that focus on the key ideas; and those that focus on the strengths and/or weaknesses.

- **Key ideas (also termed as "fundamental"/"distinctive" ideas; "key"/"significant" features)**

  In exams Jan2009, Jan2010, Jun2010, Jan2011, Jan2012 (sufficient reason), Jun2012 (evidence), Jun2013

As with the design argument, a helpful approach to this question type is to make a list of what you consider to be some of the distinctive features of the cosmological argument.

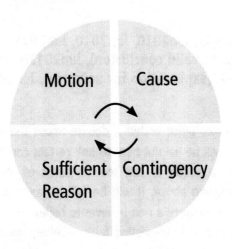

Next, link these key ideas with the views of a scholar.

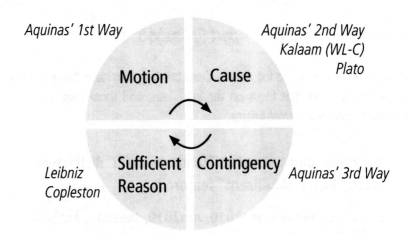

If a particular key idea is mentioned in the question, you must be prepared to explore it fully. For example, the January 2012 question asks for a discussion of the statement:

Nothing takes place without a sufficient reason.

The A-grader should conduct a detailed exploration of this idea, considering the background to it; the key thinkers (Leibniz, Swinburne); associated schools of thought involved (Kalaam, William Lane Craig), as well as the contrast with the concept of infinite regress. Try to refer to the title **AT LEAST THREE TIMES** in your answer.

▶ **Strengths and weaknesses questions**

  In exams Jun2009, Jan2013

Continue in this way, by building on your plan with details, dates, quotations, and links with similar ideas, then adding strengths and weaknesses associated with each. For example, a direct attack on the idea of "sufficient reason" which is put forward by Leibniz, and built on by Swinburne, is Russell's "brute fact"argument.

Note: Listen to the famous radio debate Copleston vs Russell, 1948, available on YouTube. Which view you accept depends on whether you think all things in the universe require an explanation, including the Big Bang, or whether you can accept Russell's argument that just because all beings have a mother does not mean the universe itself has a mother. Dawkins agrees with him, arguing that we should not ask what happened before the Big Bang, because the question does not make sense.

A twist on the traditional "key ideas" question is this one from June 2012:

Examine the evidence used to support the cosmological argument.

A way to approach this is to look at each key idea, and pull out the evidential aspect within it, for example, the evidence of cause and effect in everyday life, such as the driving of a car.

Whether the question specifically asks for both strengths and weaknesses, or just one of these categories, you must not rush your examination of the arguments. The question simply indicates which aspects to focus on, rather than which to omit completely. A solid response (both parts combined) will incorporate introduction, arguments, strengths, weaknesses and critical evaluation.

Cosmological argument - part (ii) analysis

Strengths questions - In exams Jan2009, Jun2010

Weaknesses questions - In exams Jan2010, Jun2010 (outweigh), Jan2012, Jun2012 (failure)

Existence of God questions - In exams Jan2009 (strong argument for), Jun2009 (reasonable to reject), Jan2011 (no firm conclusions), Jun2011, Jan2012 (fails as proof), Jan2013 (not convincing), Jun2013 (compelling argument)

Part (ii) questions tend to take one of two courses:

- they either ask you to weigh up the balance of strengths and weaknesses and come to a conclusion about whether the argument is fundamentally strong or weak, or

- they ask for an assessment of the argument's power to convince about the existence of God.

Reasons for rejecting the argument as a proof of the existence of God may include a discussion of the difference between probability and proof, the problem of interpretation inherent in ideas based on empirical data, and the "leap of logic" traditional versions of the argument may assume.

There may be discussion of ... the significant problems of inductive reasoning not leading to proof. (June 2011 mark scheme)

However, these considerations may equally lead someone to be agnostic about God's existence, where they have previously considered themselves atheist, or to consider that for them, a study of the argument has increased the probability of God's existence. These and others are legitimate conclusions, provided they are based on sound reasoning.

Problem of evil - part (i) analysis

▸ **Key features/characteristics**

In exams Jan2009, Jun2010, Jun2013

The questions so far have not named any key features in particular. It is, therefore, important to have a few up your sleeve that you can use to structure your answer, by linking with the main theodicies and defences. For example, how about using John Hick's terms "soul-deciding" and "soul-making" to bounce you into discussion of the Augustinian and Irenaean theodicies? Try to refer to the terms of the question **AT LEAST**

THREE TIMES in your answer, using link phrases like "A key characteristic of the next theodicy under discussion is soul-making."

▸ **Solutions and problems**

In exams Jun2009, Jan2010, Jun2010, Jan2011, Jun2011, Jan2012, Jun2012, Jan2013, Jun2013

The question never asks for more than two theodicies in part (i), probably because of time constraints. As part of your discussion of the solutions, the strengths and weaknesses need to be addressed if they are not specifically asked for in part (ii). For example, part (ii) of the June 2010 question asks the candidate to consider that the solutions presented in part (i) are "only partially successful". This means that your part (i) need not include criticisms of the solutions, as these are called for in part (ii).

Examiner Comment - When dealing with the Augustinian theodicy, don't neglect the focus on redemption through Christ's sacrifice.

Problem of evil - part (ii) analysis

Solutions questions - In exam Jan2010, Jan2011

Problems questions - In exam Jan2009 (POE can't be solved), Jun2009 (for religious belief), Jan2010, Jan2011, Jun2011, Jan2012, Jun2012, Jan2013 (obstacles to religious belief), Jun2013

Most questions ask for a discussion about whether the solutions are successful or not, or whether religious belief/the existence of God can be justified in light of the existence of evil. Steer clear of "sit on the fence" answers, which use phrases like "it depends on your point of view/ beliefs". If you are struggling to come to the conclusion that the existence of evil rules out the existence of God, then you probably think that it does not. This falls a long way short of declaring religious belief, but it does leave open the idea that God and evil can coherently and logically co-exist, which is a strong conclusion.

Miracles - part (i) analysis

▸ **Key concepts/characteristics, reasons to believe, definitions**

In exams Jan2009, Jun2009, Jan2010, Jun2010, Jan2011, Jun2011, Jan2013

Be prepared for a question that asks how Hume defines miracles (June 2009). Do not worry about other scholars being asked about specifically, as the specification indicates that while many scholars may be referred to, Hume is the only one who may be identified in questions. Therefore a very detailed grasp of his contribution is essential.

▸ **Strengths and weaknesses**

In exams Jan2012, Jun2013

If you are asked to consider the strengths and weaknesses of miracles, you need to find a way to put the arguments into this format (rather like with the key words questions).

▶ **Problems (criticisms)**

In exam Jun2012

The problems with belief in miracles are not usually discussed in part (i), but the June 2012 question is an exception. How do you approach a question that starts with the problems of believing in miracles? The mark scheme gives the following suggestions for the type of problems the A-grader might discuss:

... conceptual problems about definitions of miracle, issues of lack of probability in relation to belief in miracles, significant difficulties about the interpretation of experience.

It may therefore be appropriate to structure all the usual A01 material around these and/or other problems associated with miracles. For example, you could look at the conceptual problems of definitions of miracle, with reference to two or more definitions from prominent scholars.

Examiner Comment - One of the problems that arises from miracles is the fact that there are so many disparate definitions of miracles - an idea that needs developing. This is so much better than simply starting with a list of definitions with no particular relevance to the question.

Miracles - part (ii) analysis

Strengths & Weaknesses - In exam Jan2012

Problems - In exams Jan2009, Jun2009, Jan2010, Jun2010, Jan2011, Jun2011, Jan2013, Jun2013

Definitions - In exams Jun2011, Jan2012

Reasons to believe - In exams Jun2010, Jun2012, Jan2013

Most questions ask for evaluation of the nature and impact of problems associated with belief in miracles. The examiner expects you to look at a range of criticisms, including a number from Hume - both a priori and a posteriori - as well as some from other contributors, such as Mackie, Moore and Smart. Make sure you come to a conclusion about how convincing these criticisms are in relation to the specific terms of the question. For example, you might explore whether previously-existing religious belief makes a difference to the meaningfulness, or otherwise, of miracles.

A slightly tricky question was asked in January 2012, as it linked definitions of miracles with evaluation of strengths and weaknesses:

Comment on the view that these strengths and weaknesses depend on which definition of miracles one is using.

The mark scheme suggests you proceed with a contrast between, for example, Hume's definition and his conclusions, which are heavily influenced by his empiricism, and that of, for example, Locke. Look carefully at these definitions, and consider which one is more likely to lead to an acceptance of miracles as convincing, or otherwise.

Religion and morality

With the infrequency of questions on religion and morality, it may be tempting for candidates to avoid this topic altogether. Not so the A-grader! The A-grader will do well to reason that with many other students avoiding it, this will be a fantastic opportunity to provide the examiner with an answer that stands out from others. Furthermore, with all questions revolving around the arguments for and against the idea that morality depends upon religion, this is actually quite an easy one to prepare for.

Religion and morality - part (i) analysis

▸ **Arguments for and against the view that morality depends on religion**

Arguments for - In exams Jan2011, Jun2011, Jun2012
Arguments against - In exams Jun2009, Jun2011, Jun2012

The June 2011 question incorporates arguments both for and against in part (i), so you would need to decide whether you would like to produce a traditional-style essay where you write an introduction, followed by arguments for, then arguments against. Or the alternative is a ping-pong match, where an argument in favour, is followed up by a corresponding argument against. This interactive discussion can then be repeated for three paragraphs, so you have a conversation, rather than a more chunky approach.

For example, a presentation of the main claims of Divine Command theorists that we need a supreme being to interpret what is wrong or right, can be countered by the Euthyphro Dilemma, which makes the point that if God commands what is right or wrong, then He could command acts of grave injustice and evil. The chapter on this topic in the accompanying Revision Guide will give you more ideas on how to proceed with your next paragraph.

Religion and morality - part (ii) analysis

▶ **Arguments for and against the view that morality depends on religion**

Arguments for - In exams Jun2009, Jun2011, Jun2012
Arguments against - In exams Jan2011, Jun2011, Jun2012

An evaluation of how convincing religious morality may be (flaws and advantages of the approach) can be complemented by an assessment of the usefulness or otherwise of secular morality. A solid evaluation may answer questions such as "Which approach to morality (secular or religious) provides the most practical/most helpful/most loving guidance for moral decision making?"

Utilitarianism - part (i) analysis

▶ **Key features/ideas/concepts**

In exams - Jan2009, Jun2009, Jan2010, Jun2011, Jun2012, Jun2013

Look at the key ideas section on the design argument for a method of planning answers to these sorts of questions. It shouldn't be hard to find key ideas within utilitarianism, and link them to arguments, scholars and examples. The mark schemes make it clear that exploring the teleological/consequentialist nature of the theory is expected, as is an awareness of the background to the theory - its social context. This might be summarised in key feature terms as "democratic", because everyone counts as one. You may add, to teleological and democratic, "quality" for Mill, "preference" for Singer, and so on. It is important that you give a decent amount of space to one or more of the modern forms of Utilitarianism - Ideal, Negative or Preference Utilitarianism (see the AS Ethics Revision Guide for summaries).

Bentham and Mill are likely to feature prominently, but at this level candidates may also make reference exclusively or additionally to other forms of Utilitarianism. (June 2013 mark scheme)

▶ **Strengths and weaknesses**

Strengths - In exams Jun2010, Jan2011 (persuasive) Weaknesses - In exams Jun2010, Jan2013 (failure)

These questions are common, and should be well rehearsed. See the design argument section for a method of building your answer on the question. This basically means that you build paragraphs that link strengths with scholars, arguments and examples - even weaknesses if the questions asks for those too. This creates a more coherent answer, rather than a "clunky" approach that tags a "strengths" paragraph on to the end of a pre-rehearsed essay.

For example, a paragraph may read like this:

> *The STRENGTH of Singer's PREFERENCE UTILITARIANISM, which takes into account people's personal tastes, may be found in its INDIVIDUALISM. You only have to look at your own family to see that one person's desire to roll around in the mud on a Saturday afternoon with a bunch of broad-shouldered pals and an oddly shaped ball may be someone else's idea of hell.*
> *(Quoted from Edexcel Revision Guide, Baron & Mears)*

If the weaknesses are also asked for, then you may proceed thus:

"Yet does Preference Utilitarianism **WEAKEN** the teleological nature of the argument? ... in the comparison of ... a prisoner who prefers to be tortured and killed out of loyalty and a sense of duty, and one who prefers to give in quickly to the physical pain of a beating, there is an obvious moral distinction. Can these preferences really be given equal moral weighting? Is one preference not better than the other? If so, we are veering towards an **ABSOLUTIST (DEONTOLOGICAL) MORALITY.**" (Ibid)

Utilitarianism - part (ii) analysis

▸ **Comparison of strengths and weaknesses**

Strengths - In exams Jan2010, Jun2010 (outweigh), Jan2013 (successful), Jun2013

Weaknesses - In exams Jan2009, Jan2010 (outweigh), Jun2010, Jan2011 (outweigh), Jun2011, Jan2012, Jun2012, Jun2013 (outweigh)

As the above list shows, by far the most popular evaluation question is a comparison between strengths and weaknesses, or an assessment of whether the theory has survived criticisms (which is essentially the same thing). Therefore, part (ii) for every question apart from June 2009 can be dealt with in a very similar way, although be sure to use the exact terms of the question. For example, if you are asked whether the weaknesses outweigh the strengths, try to use the word **OUTWEIGH** at least twice during your answer. So you could start your answer with the phrase "It could be argued that the weaknesses of the argument outweigh the strengths". Follow up this sentence with a reference to what you hold to be the most convincing criticism, and which approach may be better.

Here is an example:

It could be argued that the weaknesses of the argument outweigh the strengths because one of the major flaws in this teleological approach is its failure to take into account the inability of human beings to reason effectively when their own happiness is at stake. In the heat of emotion, the lens of past experiences, and from within the climate of social expectation, how can our personal preferences really count as one? This may lead us to reject a teleological method of decision-making in favour of a more principled approach such as Kantian Deontology where the temptation to convince ourselves that fudging the truth may keep the most people happy (because we secretly don't want to own up to our misdemeanour), can be trumped by the "do not lie" principle.

The beginning of the next paragraph may then read: "However, I believe that the strengths of the theory outweigh the weaknesses because ..." One approach in response to the above argument is that you may believe in a human being's ability to detach themselves from a situation through using their own rational capability, a characteristic of human beings that Kant himself believed in! It is worth noting here that although Kantian deontology is not specifically included on the AS syllabus, it is an excellent tool for critiquing any teleological theory, and providing a comparison.

Candidates are likely to make direct reference to the wording of the question. (Examiner Report)

Finally, remember not to spew out a pre-learned response. The mark schemes and reports are teeming with encouragements to keep your answer relevant.

Situation Ethics - part (i) analysis

▸ **Key features/ideas/concepts/characteristics**

In exams Jan2009, Jan2010, Jun2010, Jun2011, Jan2012, Jun2012, Jan2013

This question type is overwhelmingly the most popular choice of examiners, so deliberate preparation for it is essential. See the design argument key features section for a working example of how to structure an answer around the key ideas or concepts. These may include its teleological nature, the relative nature of the theory, the centrality of agape (the law of love), personalism and positivism, the example of Jesus, and the attempt by Robinson and Fletcher to establish an ethic for "man come of age". It may even incorporate some strengths, such as its flexibility. Build up each concept with reference to scholars, quotations, examples and strengths, and you will have a really good answer.

Note: When using examples, you will get much more credit for using those cited by scholars, as the mark scheme makes clear:

Case studies are likely to be used with discretion, perhaps Fletcher's own, rather than hypothetical scenarios. (January 2009 mark scheme)

It will certainly be useful to read Joseph Fletcher's source material, and have two or three well-rehearsed, concise examples ready to quote.

▸ **Strengths and weaknesses questions**

In exam Jun2013

This was a new question type for 2013, and your main decision for planning a question like this is whether to structure it according to a traditional approach, or a ping-pong approach (see Part (i) analysis: Arguments for and against the view that morality depends on religion).

Situation Ethics - part (ii) analysis

▸ **Relationship with religion**

In exams Jan2009, Jun2010, Jun2013

The mark schemes are clear here that a discussion about the true nature of New Testament ethics is relevant (so do not be worried about transgressing into theology). The main debate is around whether Christians should apply Jesus's commands to love, and his rebukes of the Pharisees' emphasis on the law as a mandate to reject all absolute moral principles; whether the New Testament should be read in light of social and cultural changes; or whether some commands and moral guidelines, such as those given on the Sermon on the Mount (Matthew 5-7) should hold eternally.

▸ **How useful is it?**

In exams Jan2010, Jan2012, Jan2013

A rejection of the usefulness of the theory may include such reasons as:

... the failures of a relative theory to offer clear moral guidance, the difficulties of applying agape, the dangers of rejecting moral absolutes, and the challenges raised by contemporary critics for failure to promote traditional religious morality. (January 2012 mark scheme)

War & Peace - part (i) analysis

▸ **Just War Theory or pacifism**

Just War - In exams Jan2009, Jan2010, Jun2010, Jan2011, Jan2012, Jun2012, Jun2013

Pacifism - In exams Jun2009, Jan2010, Jun2010, Jun2011, Jan2012, Jan2013

As you can see from the list above, a consideration of the arguments for and against Just War Theory and pacifism is a necessity if you choose this topic, and why wouldn't you? It comes up every session and varies very little. The two important considerations for the A-grader are:

1. To move swiftly between a variety of thinkers, sources and examples in detail: mark schemes warn against

falling into narrative ... resorting to anecdote. (January 2009 mark scheme)

2. To make your answer your own by finding some unusual (but not obscure) philosophers, thinkers and examples to quote in your answer.

... some examples of modern warfare may be appropriately applied with careful relation to the wording of the question. (June 2012 mark scheme)

War & Peace - part (ii) analysis

▸ **Compatibility between Just War Theory and pacifism**

In exam Jun2010

This is a tricky question, and has only come up once so far, but with a bit of preparation, the A-grader could be at an advantage if this one does come up; many less-prepared candidates will steer clear of it, or ignore the terms of the question.

The exam report is not very specific here, but it seems to me that a sensible way to proceed would be to look at the principles that underlie Just War Theory and pacifism, and consider whether there is any similarity. This should not be hard to do, considering that both have theoretical foundations in Christianity, so some key themes that underpin each must be love, justice, protection for the weak, regard for God's creation, etc. It would be good to include some Bible references, scholar quotation and the out-working of the principle here, making the distinction between the two applications of that principle clear. For example, the Just War theorist will apply the "sanctity of life" principle to the need for a use of force to protect the lives of innocent civilians from violent oppression. However, the pacifist will apply the same principle as an absolute, so that any destruction of life is forbidden. I think that an exploration of the similarity and difference between these two principles would be a very interesting question to answer indeed.

▸ How "religious" are JWT and/or pacifism?

In exams Jan2010, Jun2013

Without repeating material you have already used in (i), you should emphasise the teachings that have a religious foundation or religious elements. For example, you could look at some scriptures, and recognise the apparent tension between some Old Testament passages and the writings of St Paul, with some of the teaching of Jesus and other Pauline epistles.

Additionally, you

... may raise issues of conscience ... the problems of misunderstanding or misapplying religious teaching or of following the commands of religious leaders in these matters. (June 2013 mark scheme)

One obvious example that springs to mind here is the extremist teachings of some Muslim leaders which seem to have inspired suicide bombing and other acts of terrorism, or the religious elements to the Protestant/Catholic tensions in Northern Ireland. It may be worth exploring why religion and acts of war are such a potent mix.

▸ Discussing the merits or otherwise of JWT or pacifism

JWT - In exams Jun2009, Jun2011, Jan2013
Pacifism - In exams Jan2009, Jan2011, Jun2012

This is by far the most popular part (ii) question, and it is important that it reads differently from part (i). You will do well to view Just War Theory through the eyes of modern warfare, remembering that it was largely developed before the advent of chemical or nuclear weapons.

Additionally, you may wish to consider whether there have been cultural and social shifts in thinking about war due to conscience and the nature of modern warfare.

It could be argued that asking about the weaknesses of pacifism for a part (ii) answer (as in June 2011) is really a question about the merits of Just War Theory. Just make sure that you show you understand that link in your response, rather than re-writing the question altogether.

Here is a good way to start: "Pacifism is a difficult position to hold because many philosophers argue that justice can sometimes best be served by going to war ..." Continue this response with reference to scholars and examples, but keep in mind that this is an evaluation question, so knowledge and understanding is not enough; you must assess the merits of this claim and decide whether you agree with it.

Sexual ethics - part (i) analysis

▸ **Dilemmas and solutions**

In exams Jan2009, Jun2009 (clear judgments about right and wrong), Jan2010, Jun2010, Jan2011, Jun2011, Jan2012 (two), Jun2012, Jan2013, Jun2013 (two)

The questions ask for no more than two dilemmas (of marital, non-marital and extra-marital sex, homosexuality and divorce, so do not feel the need to prepare thoroughly on more than that). However, I have had students in the past who have been caught out by a question like the one of June 2011, that asked for discussion of just one issue; you must have sufficient detail about one issue in particular, in case you are given this limitation.

Sexual ethics - part (ii) analysis

▸ **Dilemmas and solutions**

In exams Jun2011 (one), Jan2012

Weighing up whether particular approaches help to solve particular dilemmas is an important aspect of this discussion. For example, if you have included Situation Ethics as a solution to the debate about marriage and divorce, then you can use some concise reference to case studies to justify your answer.

... *candidates are likely to be able to distinguish clearly between "problems" and "dilemmas". (January 2012 mark scheme)*

▶ **Relationship with religion (is it helpful or relevant in solving dilemmas?)**

In exams Jan2009, Jun2009, Jan2010, Jan2011, Jun2012, Jan2013

This is clearly the examiners' most popular question in sexual ethics, and it pays to have prepared a chart of strengths and weaknesses of the role religion plays in this debate. Be prepared to say whether, on balance, you think it is or isn't relevant or helpful in solving dilemmas. You may like to make distinctions between different types of dilemmas (eg divorce or homosexuality), or different applications of dilemma (eg for individuals, groups within religion, or society and law-making).

▶ **Freedom of choice (is this the most important thing?)**

In exams Jun2010, Jun2013

Mark schemes are clear that it is appropriate to give your own "informed opinion" about this. A poor answer might go along these lines:

I feel that freedom of choice is the most important consideration because it depends on your point of view.

This is not informed! A much better response might be:

On balance, FREEDOM OF CHOICE appears to me to be THE MOST IMPORTANT CONSIDERATION because a religious person believes in free will. For example, the QUR'AN says "there is no coercion in religion". Furthermore, a NON-RELIGIOUS PERSON will consider themselves beholden to no supreme authority, and therefore responsible for their own actions. So whether you are religious or not, freedom of choice is ESSENTIAL to this debate.

UNIT 2 INVESTIGATIONS (EDEXCEL 6RS02)

AREA B - THE STUDY OF PHILOSOPHY OF RELIGION (EDEXCEL 6RS02/1B)

1. Religious experience; meditation

> **Contribution of 1 or more scholars/studies**
>
> **In exam Jan2010**

The most able candidates produce original arguments and write in a fluent and interesting way, covering a variety of scholars other than, or including, the most popular - Swinburne and James. Disappointing responses are those which describe the views, rather than using the views to support points made about the topics under exploration. Good answers look at the relationship with God today, as well as eschatological considerations and their impact. Examiners seem to like answers which incorporate less popular material, such as non-Christian religious experiences.

> **Illuminate/Particularly revealing/Transforming for understanding of ourselves and God**
>
> **In exams Jun2009, Jun2010, Jan2012, Jun2012, Jun2013**

Interesting scholarship mentioned in exam reports includes the Psychology of Religion material (such as Freud, Jung, Eliade), Persinger's God helmet, existentialism, and the work of Otto. However, the reports warn against an over-reliance on Persinger's helmet, narrative material about miracles, or case studies of near-death experiences. Case studies, where used critically, were recommended, and St Teresa, Julian of Norwich, the Toronto Blessing and conversion experiences were mentioned as good choices. In addition to the above, critics other than Hume should also be included, although there is some criticism of presenting the work of sceptics such as Richard Dawkins as narrative, rather than critically evaluated.

The best responses evaluated and referred to the question consistently through their response. Examiner Report, June 2012

‣ **God only known through communication**

In exam Jan2011

This question asks you to consider the word "only", so do not ignore it. In addition to the points raised above, you may wish to consider whether there are other ways to know the divine, such as through holy scriptures, experience of the natural world, revelation through prophets, or whether these are also forms of communication.

‣ **Religious experience just ordinary experience with religious interpretation/all in the mind**

In exams Jun2011, Jan2013

A good example of attempting this question may consider categories of religious experiences that rely more on individual interpretation, and perhaps others that may be harder to classify as "all in the mind". These concepts should then be linked with the work of particular scholars and examples. An example of the former may be answers to prayer, as discussed by Caroline Franks Davis. And the latter, the communal experience category of Swinburne, where it is harder to confine experience to the mind of an individual.

2. Contrasting standpoints on the relationship between mind and body

▸ **Mind and body are the same thing or different/range of possibilities for explaining mind and body relationship**

In exams Jun2010, Jun2011, Jan2012, Jun2012, Jun2013

The strongest answers have a clear grasp of the historical and cultural context of the scholars they are referring to, for example pre- and post-enlightenment thinkers. There are many key terms to employ in this subject area, and it is important that key terms such as dualism, monism, and materialism are swiftly linked with scholars from that field, for example, Dawkins with materialism, Descartes with dualism. Material about life after death can be used here, but it must be related to the question. Scholars who are mentioned in reports as wide-ranging are Descartes, Plato, Aristotle and Ryle, and particular note is given to candidates who focus on Greek philosophy particularly well.

▸ **Never fully be understood/Difficult to account for relationship**

In examsJun2009, Jan2010

This is essentially quite similar to the above, but the claim needs to be addressed. One way to go is to consider that religious responses rely on our ability to comprehend the divine, a claim that some religious scholars would challenge, namely Augustine who believed firmly in God's transcendence. An interesting scripture to explore is 1 Corinthians 13:12, which could be used to support either conclusion ... enjoy!

▸ **Essential for understanding personal identity**

In exam Jan2011

Not surprisingly, the main comment made in addition to more general comments about exam technique was that weaker candidates failed to apply their material to a discussion of personal identity. A good example of discussion will consider whether deciding on dualism or monism matters. One good example applied this debate to the case study of a person who has suffered an accident, and subsequently, their body changes considerably. Does this affect their essence? You need to make up your mind on the importance of these concepts for understanding who you are, and to do so, you can draw on helpful material in religious texts, and original sources, for example the Bible, the work of Darwin and Psychology.

Examiner Tip - "Your conclusion can be strengthened if you can answer the question by a final statement that summarises the thrust of your essay." (Examiners Report, January 2011)

▸ **All three (choice: mind, personal identity, the soul)**

In exam Jan2013

For a choice question, make sure that you state clearly in the introduction which concept or concepts you have chosen to write about, and stick firmly to that. One way to approach this question is to consider all three in turn, and decide which concept best illuminates the debate, or whether a combination of two or more is most helpful. You may like to consider the anti-realist approach to explaining the meaning of certain terms used within religion; they may make sense to people within those spheres of thought, but do they carry any meaning for those outside particular frames of reference? Look up the views of Wittgenstein.

There are two tricky questions here: the June 2012 question asks you to consider that "the mind is the brain and no more", and similarly, the June 2013 question asks you to consider that the "mind is more than the brain". These are essentially questions about dualism and monism, and they ask you specifically to explore whether we are basically just matter or whether there is more to us. Are we "bytes and bytes and bytes of digital information" (Richard Dawkins, River Out Of Eden), or are we "flesh-animated-by-soul" (JAT Robinson)? Or put more lyrically, "Are we human, or are we dancer?" (Human, The Killers). Therefore, focus your discussion on the monism-dualism debate, and use the identical terms of the question.

3. A study of one or more philosophers of religion

▸ **Distinctive contribution/significant features (and how far this may have influenced philosophical thought)**

In exams Jun2009, Jun2010, Jan2013

The biggest warning for very general questions like these is against offering a biographical account of an author, without critique, analysis or reference to the question. It seems from the reports that one of the most interesting ways of tackling this question is to pick two scholars who have similar or contrasting ideas, such as Kierkegaard and Sartre, but the variety of combinations is vast, and the examiner will delight in reading a study of an original combination. It is important that you choose a scholar or scholars you find interesting; enthusiasm for the topic area was praised.

Examiner Tip - "The best answers referred to a range of ideas or works by the chosen philosopher and put them in the correct context of their time or the impact on subsequent thought which made for interesting, thoughtful and scholarly analysis of their ideas." (Examiner Report, June 2013)

Although the question asks you to focus on one or more scholars in this particular area, the A-grader will certainly employ the views of a number of scholars who have something to say about their chosen scholar's work. For example, Swinburne's endorsement of Leibniz's work on the principle of sufficient reason, and Russell's critique of it, will be helpful in your assessment of the contribution of Leibniz's thought.

▸ **Philosophical understanding of a theme hindered or helped (or given insight by) a particular scholar or scholars**

In exams Jan2010, Jun2010, Jan2012, Jun2013

In assessing whether the contribution of a scholar has helped or hindered, it may be useful to ask some particular questions, such as:

- Is there any logical error in the thinking of x?

- Was the thinking of x appropriate in their day, but no longer relevant in the modern world?

- Can the thinking of x be applied helpfully to any modern issues, such as medical ethics?

- To what extent do the criticisms or weaknesses of the scholar's views on y, impact on the strength of his or her thinking?

- Which other scholars have been influenced by the thinking of x?

(What is his or her legacy?)

- … and so on …

▸ **Significant challenges posed by (Jan 2011)/provokes considerable debate (June 2012)**

In exams Jan2011, Jun2012

Avoid organising your answer around arguing for and against the existence of God, rather than the question. For a question like this, you would do well to present the case that significant challenges are posed by the philosophy of x, and contrast this critique with the idea that many challenges within philosophy are helped or solved by the philosophy of x. Make sure you come to a conclusion about which side of the debate you would come down on. Likewise, with the charge "provokes considerable debate" you could contrast this side with the idea that the thinking of x (or x and y), provokes considerable consensus of opinion among certain areas of philosophical thought.

With any question, it is important to find the bone of contention, the point of controversy, or an angle for critique; this makes an essay interesting, and aids evaluation.

AREA C - THE STUDY OF ETHICS (EDEXCEL 6RS02/1C)

1. Medical ethics

A sure way to miss the A grade is to answer the wrong question! It is worth my saying again that the questions come up in the same order every time, so if you have prepared a medical ethics topic, then you will answer the first question on your paper (question 1).

Examiner Comment - "At least 10% of the responses for (question 3) were actually responses more suited to question 1 on medical ethics." (June 2010)

▸ **Developments should/should not be guided by religious principles**

In exams Jun2009, Jun2010, Jun2011, Jan2012, Jun2012, Jan2013

The most obvious way to tackle this question will be to consider why philosophers might argue that religious principles should, and contrast that with why they should not, guide developments in medical ethics, before coming to a developed personal conclusion.

Reasons suggested in past questions as to why developments should not be guided by religious principles are:

- They are old-fashioned. (January 2013)

- They are a hindrance. (June 2011)

It is important to notice that question 1 uses the phrase "religious principles **ALONE**". Hence it would be perfectly legitimate to agree with the statement, while arguing that religious principles are not old-fashioned.

With these questions it is very important to recognise that everyone, whether religious or not, adheres to a particular context within which they make informed choices. Rather than implying that religion is biased or obviously flawed, it would be better to recognise that "personal choice is usually under the guiding scrutiny of a secular or religious principle that is being adhered to" (Examiner's Report, January 2013). So the contrast between deontological/objectivist ethics and teleological/consequentialist ethics is a much more scholarly debate.

Examiner Tip - "Strong opinions in the matter of personal choice destroyed many candidates' objectivity in writing, and many candidates were arguing that religion is a problem simply because it gets in our way." (January, 2013)

Abortion is obviously a very popular topic here, and the examiner reports praised explorations of organ transplants and stem cell research/embryology as "memorable".

If your chosen topic is abortion or euthanasia, then you need to make every effort to make your essay stand out from others and move well beyond GCSE material.

Instead of merely walking down the well-worn paths of Situation Ethics and Utilitarianism here, you could apply, for example, Aristotle's virtue ethics and Aquinas's natural law in the for/against debate. Furthermore, it would be advisable to have some contemporary examples of thinking and case studies from which to draw.

Studies that reflect the less travelled path often stand out from the crowd in terms of achievement if the material is substantive, up-to-date and deployed effectively to argue a viewpoint. (Examiner's Report, June 2013)

▸ Religious/ethical responses to issues

In exams Jan2010 (controversies and how far they resolve OR conflict with religious or moral principles), Jan2011, Jun2013 (variety confusing)

You might do well to include different religious or ethical concepts, such as sanctity of life and freedom of choice, and organise your answer around those, linking them with particular theories, scholars and examples. However it is also important to be aware of the historical and cultural context for these responses, which requires wider reading and clearer understanding, for example:

Situation Ethics was commonly identified as a secular approach and its Protestant Episcopalian origins largely ignored. (Examiner's Report, January 2013)

The A-grader will recognise that there is a wide variety of thinking that has drawn on religious principles, and also that there is a wide variety of thinking within different areas of religious and secular ethics. The best answers distinguished between closely related responses, such as Act and Rule Utilitarianism; Catholic thinking based on scripture, and that based on Natural Moral Law, which is grounded in reason; and different approaches within Islam.

2. The natural world

Examiners would like to see more students selecting this question, and not just writing on the issue of animal welfare; they see site recycling, vegetarianism, genetic engineering, habitat conservation and the marine rights bill as hugely interesting areas with wide-ranging repercussions for the stewardship debate. A wide-range of scholars and ethical/religious approaches should be explored in relation to the question and the issue(s) selected. These may include Situation Ethics, St Francis of Assisi, Singer, Spinoza, Robinson, papal documents and biblical material including the books of Genesis, the Psalms, the teaching of Jesus Christ, and the book of Revelation.

▸ **Greed and Stewardship contrast**

In exams Jun2009, Jun2012, Jan2013

There is an example on the Edexcel website (Examiner Report, June 2011) which shows some good practice, including:

- deployment of a range of accurate vocabulary, eg intrinsic value; anthropocentricism; industrialisation; fundamentalist; rapture; hierarchy; consumerism

- focus on the greed vs stewardship debate

- moving swiftly through case studies and examples which back up clearly-made points, rather than stand-alone narrative

- relevant use of statistics to back up or introduce a point

- a direct answer to the question of impossibility.

▶ Religious/moral significance of stewardship

In exams Jan2010, Jun2010, Jan2011, Jun2011 (impossible challenge), Jan2012 (positive guide), Jun2013 (dominion, not stewardship)

Examiners like responses about stewardship to be focused on the question, covering a range of views about stewardship and using modern environmental/ecological issues. Always find ways to link these back to key debates, as well as religious, moral and/or secular ethical approaches. For example, there were some essays on the 2010 oil disaster and this was related to the idea of dominion versus domination which could also be linked to Peter Singer's Preference Utilitarianism.

Examiner Tip - A good introduction could set out some key ideas related to stewardship and how the candidate thinks an ethical theory might contribute a useful working principle for developing good stewardship. (June 2010)

3. Equality in the modern world

All questions use the phrase "in the modern world", and popular choices of issues were racism (especially Martin Luther King and Malcolm X) and homosexuality, although there have been some good essays on "speciesism" and animal rights. (Be aware here, though, that the latter may not be best suited to question 2: the natural world.) Examiners would like to see more essays on sexism and women's rights.

Examiner Tip - "It would be good to see some real case studies being used with some exploration of recent legal developments that might stimulate the debate." (June 2010)

▸ **Equality established or equality is only possible with Religious / Ethical principles**

In exams Jan2010, Jun2010, Jan2011

Examiners are weary of answers that seem to view religion as altogether controlling and outdated, or those which are overly emotional or opinionated. The A-grader should be careful to make distinctions between ethical viewpoints within religious traditions, and whether they are deontological or teleological in nature, absolutist or relativist. The best answers looked for different viewpoints and ethical approaches within religious traditions, for example, "better answers on homosexuality seemed to have current knowledge of the Anglican debate over Gene Robinson and the threat of splits in the Anglican Communion" (Examiner's Report, January 2010).

- **Issues that challenge equality (including religious / ethical principles and practices)**

  In exams Jun2009, Jan2012, Jun2012, Jan2013, Jun2013

In an exemplar essay, a student argued that "Catholicism's abhorrence of homosexuality should be eclipsed by Jesus' mantra to 'love thy neighbour as thyself'" (Examiner's Report, January 2010). This is a good example of a recognition of contrasting approaches within religion, as well as concise explanation containing a solid grasp of philosophical terminology.

Freedom of choice should not be used as a justification in and of itself, but needs to be related to, and contrasted with, scholarship and thought traditions, for example, Preference Utilitarianism and Divine Command Theory.

- **Religious/Ethical principles only possible if equality upheld**

  In exam Jun2011

Through application to the topic you have chosen, you need to consider whether Religion and Ethics should uphold equality, through an in-depth study of concepts and teachings within these areas. If equality is not essential to the principles inherent in some religions, then you need to show why, rather than assuming that equality is (self-evidently) an ideal that must be upheld by virtue of itself.

How to prepare for the examination

You need to write answers on **THREE TOPICS**.

You have **1¾ HOURS** in the exam (**35 MINUTES** per question).

If you are only studying Philosophy of Religion and Ethics, you can either complete:

- two questions from Philosophy and one from Ethics, or

- two from Ethics and one from Philosophy.

PHILOSOPHY OF RELIGION

You should choose three topics from separate bullet points. Some topics within bullet points may be combined, so you should have at least a loose grasp of the whole bullet point, in the event of a combination question.

- The design argument

- The cosmological argument

- The problem of evil and suffering

- Miracles

ETHICS

- The relationship between religion and morality

- Utilitarianism

- Situation Ethics (you need two of these first three as one will not come up)

- Issues of war and peace

- Sexual ethics

MAKING REVISION NOTES

The following notes are helpful for a basic grasp of the main descriptive and evaluative points for each of the topics covered. They are also a guide for how to structure revision notes. Some topics are not included; try to construct your own for these areas.

As an A-grade student, you will need to add layers of detail from your notes and essays to gain credit in the higher levels, but you can use these pointers as building blocks for well-structured points. Don't be nervous about substituting scholars or points here for your own ideas: examiners hate trawling through identical material, so use the following as a tool, and make it your own.

UNIT 1: FOUNDATIONS

Philosophy of Religion

You can either focus on the **DESIGN ARGUMENT** or the **COSMOLOGICAL ARGUMENT**.

1a) The design (teleological) arguments

▸ **Introduction**

- Empirical argument - Based on sensory evidence.

- A posteriori arguments - Those which depend on some kind of evidence to support them.

- Inductive reasoning - Making inferences and drawing general conclusions from particular examples.

- A summary quote or basic outline of the argument's essence.

▸ **Key scholars**

- **ARISTOTLE** - Postulated that all natural objects have a purpose and a reason for their existence.

- **THOMAS AQUINAS** (13th C) - Fifth of the "Five Ways" of demonstrating God's existence. He used the example of an archer shooting an arrow at a target to suggest that nothing is purposeful without the aid of a "guiding hand".

- **WILLIAM PALEY** (18th C) - Just as one may find a watch on a heath and conclude, from its workings, that someone had designed it rather than that it appeared through chance, so everything in the universe is clearly designed.

▸ **Critique**

- **DAVID HUME** -

  1. The universe appears ordered, but not designed; "design" is a loaded term.

  2. To say that the universe appears to be designed so God is behind it is a leap of logic. Why not say it is a team of gods, a foreign god or an infant deity?

- **JS MILL** - This universe is not the product of a benevolent, omnipotent God. Suffering indicates malfunction in the design. He concludes that God is not all-powerful.

- **RICHARD DAWKINS** - Darwinian evolution by natural selection gives an alternative answer to the question why are things so good at doing what they do? They have gradually become better suited to their purpose, as the survival of the fittest ensures that only the strong survive. "The mature Darwin blew it (the design argument) out of the water."

▸ **Conclusion**

- Some think the argument fails - they agree with Dawkins that natural selection completely explains why things are so good at doing what they do: we no longer need God.

- **RATIONALISTS** do not accept empirical arguments.

- Others think the argument succeeds and can be re-formulated in light of scientific developments (theistic evolution): FR Tennant's (1866-1957) **AESTHETIC PRINCIPLE** suggests that "biologically superfluous" beauty shows design. His **ANTHROPIC PRINCIPLE** refers to the observation that the universe is "finely tuned" so that life will inevitably occur.

- **DEISTS** accept the anthropic principle, but agree with Mill that God can no longer be involved.

1 b) The cosmological (causation) argument

▸ **Introduction**

- Empirical argument - Based on sensory evidence.

- A posteriori arguments - Those which depend on some kind of evidence to support them.

- Inductive reasoning - Making inferences and drawing general conclusions from particular examples.

- A summary quote or basic outline of the argument's essence.

▸ **Key scholars**

- **PLATO AND ARISTOTLE** (4th C BC) - Postulated the need for a craftsman and a cause of all things.

- **THOMAS AQUINAS** (13th C) First three of his "five ways" -

proofs of the existence of God: **MOTION** - "It is necessary to arrive at a first mover, moved by no other, and this we call God." **CAUSE** - "It is necessary to admit a first efficient cause to which everyone gives the name God." **CONTINGENCY** - "We cannot but admit the existence of some being having of itself its'own necessity, and not receiving it from another ... This all men speak of as God."

- **THE KALAAM ARGUMENT** - "It is an axiom of reason that all that comes to be must have a reason to bring it about. The world has come to be. Ergo the world must have a cause to bring it about."(Al-Ghazali) William Lane Craig developed this idea, using the analogy of a library with an infinite number of books to show that infinity cannot exist in actuality.

▸ **Critique**

- **DAVID HUME** - Aquinas is guilty of an inductive leap of logic: just because we can demonstrate the need for a necessary being does not mean it is the God of classical theism.

- **BERTRAND RUSSELL** - Builds on Hume's criticisms: perhaps the universe is its own "brute fact" (infinite regression). "I should say that the universe is just there, and that is all." Furthermore, just because every human being has a mother does not mean the universe itself has a mother.

- **SCIENCE** - Some microscopic particles are thought to exist without a cause (Quantum Mechanics).

▸ Conclusion

Some think the cosmological argument succeeds:

- **COPLESTON** argued with Russell (radio debate, 1948 - see YouTube) that infinite regression cannot explain the overall cause of the universe. "If you add up chocolates to infinity you get chocolates after all and not a sheep ... So if you add up contingent beings to infinity, you still get contingent beings, not a necessary being."

- **LEIBNIZ'S PRINCIPLE** of sufficient reason - There must be a complete explanation. Infinite regression is not a complete explanation. (If he were alive today he may say neither is the Big Bang - we can still ask what caused the Big Bang.)

Others think it fails:

- Rationalists do not think sensory evidence is trustworthy; **DESCARTES'** malicious demon.

- Even if we accept the need for a cause, there are no grounds to think that the explanation we're looking for is God (inductive leap of logic). **PETER ATKINS** believes science is "steadily and strenuously working toward a comprehensible explanation".

2. The problem of evil and suffering

▸ Introduction

- "My God, my God, why have you forsaken me?" (Psalm 22:1)

- The Inconsistent Triad was put forward by **JL MACKIE** - If God is omnipotent, he would be able to stop suffering. If God is benevolent, he would want to stop suffering. Evil exists, therefore God cannot be both benevolent and omnipotent.

- Natural evil is evil not caused by humans, eg earthquakes.

- Moral evil is evil caused by humans, eg murder.

- A theodicy is an attempt to justify God's existence and attributes in the face of evil.

▸ The Augustinian Theodicy

- **ST AUGUSTINE** of Hippo (354-430) based his theodicy on classical thought: Plato's "Forms" (everything on Earth is an imperfect representation of its perfection) and scripture: God created everything, and it was "very good". (Genesis 1:31)

- Evil is therefore in the world because of "the Fall" (Genesis 3). Evil is a privato boni, a privation (or absence) of the good, not a real quality.

- This theory is known as soul-deciding: the misuse of free will leads to suffering and death.

- **STRENGTH** - It encourages human beings to take responsibility for their own wrong-doing.

- **WEAKNESS** - Evil seems much more than just an absence of good, eg absence of love is indifference, not hate.

▶ The Irenaean Theodicy

- **IRENAEUS** (AD 130-202) saw evil as a purposeful reality: evil helps us to appreciate good.

- Free will is part of our being made in God's own image and likeness (Genesis 1:26). Without it we would be puppets.

- John **HICK** agreed, and called the world a "vale of soul-making". Everyone will eventually reach heaven; we cannot see now how evil fits into the great scheme of things, but after death, it will all work out for the best. This is called eschatological fulfilment.

- **STRENGTH** - It recognises the role of suffering in human development, eg overcoming a disability.

- **WEAKNESS** - The distribution and intensity of evil - some suffer more than others.

▶ Process Theology

- **AN WHITEHEAD** was the inspiration for this solution, which sees God as acting within the spatio-temporal realm - suffering and working alongside us.

- God cannot force our choices, but we have free will to make our own decisions.

- **DAVID GRIFFIN** supports this, arguing that it is logically impossible for God to prevent moral evil. The idea that he can is known as the **OMNIPOTENCE FALLACY**.

- **STRENGTH** - This keeps God's benevolence intact and has scriptural back-up - Emmanuel.

- **WEAKNESS** - This seems to challenge God's omnipotence and other parts of scripture - "God in Heaven".

▶ **Conclusion**

Choose your position, showing why you reject the others:

- One is better than the others - Explain why, using strengths and weaknesses above.

- All fail - DZ Phillips argues that a God who planned evil for good would be an evil god.

- Combination - The solution to this complex question is most likely to be a complex one.

Ethics

You need to cover two of the following three: Religion and Morality; Utilitarianism; Situation Ethics.

1b) Utilitarianism

▶ **Introduction**

- A teleological approach to ethics.

- Relative - morality is dependent on circumstances.

- Consequentialist - The consequences of an action solely determine whether it is the right thing to do.

- Often summarised by the Principle of Utility - "the greatest good for the greatest number".

▶ **Key scholars**

- **JEREMY BENTHAM (ACT)** - Hedonist - "Nature has placed mankind under the governance of two sovereign masters, pain and pleasure." (1823) Established the Hedonic Calculus - which could be used to establish whether an action promoted pleasure over pain.

- **JOHN STUART MILL (RULE)** - Criticised Bentham's simplistic view of pleasure. Rather than a purely quantitative assessment of pleasure and pain Mill argued that a qualitative approach was needed - introduced higher and lower pleasures. A reason for this was to try and prevent the justification of immoral actions (which was possible under Act Utilitarianism). Also introduces "harm principle" to protect the minority.

- **PETER SINGER (PREFERENCE)** - This modern-day approach argues that the right action is one that maximises the preferences that individual human beings make in life. Rejects Mill's approach, which could be considered "elitist".

▶ **Critique**

- Deontologists - including **IMMANUEL KANT** - reject Utilitarianism's willingness to use humans as a means to an end. Approach also highlights problems with predicting consequences. Argues that some actions are intrinsically wrong, eg murder, rape.

- Christians - Utilitarianism could easily be used to justify actions that go against biblical teaching - eg it denies the sanctity of life.

- **ROBERT NOZICK** (1938-2002) criticises Bentham's hedonism - Do pleasurable experiences lead to human contentment?

- **RICHARD DAWKINS** would reject the theory's optimistic view of humanity's ability to apply the principle of utility and argues that human behaviour is heavily determined by genes.

▸ **Conclusion**

- Some think that the argument fails because of its failure to rule out any actions as intrinsically right or wrong - deontological argument.

- Others argue that the theory is applicable to difficult modern ethical dilemmas and is in keeping with our culturally relative times - teleological/relative argument.

- You need to decide how valid the theory is and specify which version/approach is most convincing and why (It would be helpful to include some additional scholarship, evidence or a quotation to illustrate your conclusion).

1c) Situation Ethics

▸ **Introduction**

- A teleological approach to ethics - Although based on single law of love.

- Relative - Morality is dependent on circumstances.

- Consequentialist - The consequences of an action solely determine whether it is the right thing to do.

- Situation Ethics takes agape love as the test of all moral actions.

- Claims to be a Christian ethic.

- Context - Time of social/cultural change in the 1960s.

▸ **Key Scholars**

- **JOSEPH FLETCHER** (1905-1991) - Situation Ethics is a middle way between legalism and antinomianism.

  - Justifies the theory by referring to the love that Jesus commanded Luke 10:27 - the greatest commandment and Jesus's criticism of the Pharisees and their over-emphasis on the law, at the expense of love (see Luke 11:37-54).

  - Offers guidance on how to apply agape love through four working principles and six fundamental principles.

- **JAT ROBINSON** - Book "Honest to God" - which also influences Fletcher - sets out basis for Situation Ethics.

▶ **Critique: who disagrees?**

- Many Christians (particularly Roman Catholics and evangelicals) - for the reason that the theory can overturn biblical commands if serving the interests of agape.

- Undermines authority of scripture - "This is the love of God, that we keep His commandments. And His commandments are not burdensome." (I John 5:3)

- Also Jesus said the following in Matthew 5:17: "Do not think that I have come to abolish the Law or the Prophets; I have not come to abolish them but to fulfil them."

- Pope Pius XII - who banned Situation Ethics from being taught in Catholic seminaries in 1954.

- Deontologists - including Immanuel Kant - who argued that actions were intrinsically right or wrong regardless of circumstances.

- And, more importantly, Aquinas and Natural Moral Law would have opposed the theory because it had the potential to go against God's intended purpose for creation - as revealed in the Bible - which was considered immoral.

- In addition consider all the standard criticisms of teleological/relative theories.

▸ Conclusion

- Some think Situation Ethics helps with decision-making - It is a guide that elevates motive over principle (strengths of Situation Ethics as a teleological theory).

- Can the theory really be considered a Christian ethic?

- Are Utilitarianism or Deontological Ethics more useful approaches to moral decision-making than Situation Ethics? If so, why?

2b) War and peace

In this topic you need to consider how moral philosophers have attempted to resolve issues surrounding war and peace.

Can wars ever be justified? Or is pacifism the most morally convincing position?

▸ Just War Theory

A Christian attempt to outline the conditions for when a war can be justified

- History/Origins - Early Church was pacifist because of its interpretation of Jesus's life and teachings, eg Jesus's condemnation of Peter for defending him violently in the Garden of Gethsemane.

- Christianity becomes the religion of the Roman Empire under Constantine.

- St Augustine and later St Aquinas develop Just War Theory.

- Jus ad Bellum and Jus in Bello - outline when war should be fought and conduct in war (have examples).

▶ Strengths of Just War

- Christians should fight against evil - "All it takes for triumph of evil is for good men to do nothing" (Edmund Burke).

- St Paul teaches that Christians should accept the authority of governments (Romans 13).

- In the long term it might be the most loving response (Fletcher and Situation Ethics).

▶ Weaknesses/Criticisms

- Breaks Decalogue - "Thou shall not kill" - Exodus 20 - sanctity of life.

- Do conflicts meet all the conditions of the theory, eg Iraq?

▶ Pacifism

- For Christians, based on the teachings of Jesus, how is this position morally justified?

- Know different types - including relative, nuclear, absolute.

- Modern example - Quakers.

- **STRENGTH** - Protects sanctity of life - Immanuel Kant - avoids using humans as a means to an end.

- **WEAKNESS** - Utilitarians - could more people suffer in the long-term from not going to war? (Mill)

▸ **Evaluation: Which approach do you consider to be more convincing?**

- From a religious perspective.

- From a moral perspective - absolute approach (all wars are wrong) vs relative; depends on the circumstances.

2a) Sexual ethics

For this topic you often need to consider two issues within sexual ethics and attempts to resolve the morality of these issues. These could be sex outside marriage, divorce or homosexuality.

▸ **Introduction**

- Outline of issues and definitions for key ideas.

- Explanations of key debate between adopting an absolute approach (often linked to religion) and a relative approach (often secular but could incorporate Situation Ethics and liberal parts of the church) to each of these issues.

▸ **Main body**

- Churches' approach to sex outside marriage/divorce - absolute.

- Churches' (particularly Catholic) view on this issue is often seen as absolute because morality is taken from the Bible which is given by God and therefore true for all time, eg the "one flesh principle" from Genesis - "You shall not commit adultery" (Exodus 20).

- Aquinas and Natural Moral Law - Everything has a God-given purpose: the primary purpose of sex is procreation.

- Other Christian scholars - Theologians, eg John Stott.

▸ **Catechisms of the Catholic Church**

- Immanuel Kant - Use the categorical imperative to establish what is intrinsically right and wrong, eg principle of universalisability.

▸ **Secular and Liberal Christian attitude towards sex outside marriage and divorce - relative**

- Apply Utilitarianism and Situation Ethics to these issues.

- Principle of Utility bases the morality of sex outside of marriage on the greatest good for the greatest number (consider possible implications of this view).

- Situations Ethics and its use of agape love to determine morality.

▸ **Evaluation: (try to add some scholarship to each point)**

- Arguments in favour of religious absolutist sexual ethics - If humans were created by God, then surely he designed their sexual organs for a purpose. Mere pleasure ignores God's intentions (love, childbirth).

- Sex is a sacred activity.

- Since the sexual revolution of the 1960s, Britain has witnessed increased numbers of teenage pregnancies and sexually transmitted infections. Fixed moral and religious rules would have lessened these problems.

- Rule Utilitarianism might support religious and absolutist principles. For example, as a general rule, adultery inflicts pain and brings a poor quality of pleasure. Thus, it is wrong.

▶ **Arguments in favour of a relativist approach to sexual ethics**

- Non-marital sex can be an expression of real love; why have rules against it?

- The Bible, Qur'an etc can be rejected as moral codes; why not choose our own ethics?

- Traditional sexual morality developed in pre-modern societies, when people got married in their teens. This is simply not relevant to today's world.

- But people are worried that a relativist view of sexual ethics will lead to a permissive society. Some people believe that there are aspects of sexuality, such as rape and paedophilia, that are objectively morally wrong and that there should be absolute rules to prevent them.

- But, some people argue that an absolute ethical approach to sexuality is repressive. In countries where Roman Catholicism is the dominant religion, contraception is often forbidden, leading to unwanted pregnancies and higher incidence of STIs.

Revision tips

TOP REVISION TIPS - UNIT 1

If you are short of time in learning for Unit 1, opt for two Philosophy of Religion questions (one argument and one issue), as each topic comes up on its own every year. Follow this up with an applied ethical issue (war and peace or sexual ethics), as they too always come up, unlike the religion and morality/Situation Ethics/utilitarianism questions where you have a two-in-three chance of your preferred topic coming up.

Make detailed revision plans/cards for each topic selected, making sure you have covered enough areas to guarantee three questions in the examination.

Make vocabulary lists or cards for each of the topics you are studying. Put the key word on one side, and the definition and context on the other. Learn them by reading them through a few times, then using the word as a trigger for the definition.

Go for a walk (fresh air helps revision!) and get someone to test you.

Get hold of as many past question papers as you can from your teacher or the Edexcel website.

Create essay plans using the tips for how to structure question types, found in the "how to analyse past exam questions" section of this book.

Practice writing essays under strict exam conditions: 35 minutes (unless you get extra time, then add 25%); no notes; no distractions.

Swap them with an aspiring A-grader classmate, and mark them, using the examiners' comments on question types included in the above section, as well as the levels descriptors on p117 of the specification (available to download from the Edexcel website).

Keep doing it, and you will improve and be ready to face any question without surprise or panic!

TOP REVISION TIPS - UNIT 2

Make sure your notes contain some original material; this is very important to examiners.

Have a few key concepts and a few quotations in mind that you would like to consider including in your introduction, but make sure it addresses the question from the outset, and therefore guides the whole piece. Be careful of length; half to three-quarters of a side should suffice.

Complete essays plans for each of the common question types you can see in the grids above: let the question guide your structure.

Practise writing answers to past questions under exam conditions, paying strict attention to time limits (1 hour 15 minutes).

Practise summarising your case studies in short paragraphs, so that they don't become long rambling blocks of narrative.

Lastly, get some sleep, be thankful to all those around you who are supporting you through this time, and really go for it - you have weeks and weeks of holiday time ahead and it is a wonderful feeling to pass it knowing that you have done your best.

Postscript

Laura Mears read PPE at Trinity College, Oxford, after which she taught in, and headed up, the Religious Studies department at Dean Close School, Cheltenham (2003-2012). She is taking a break from full-time teaching in order to raise a family; toddler Gilbert and bump.

Lightning Source UK Ltd.
Milton Keynes UK
UKOW05f1937260914

239231UK00001BA/8/P